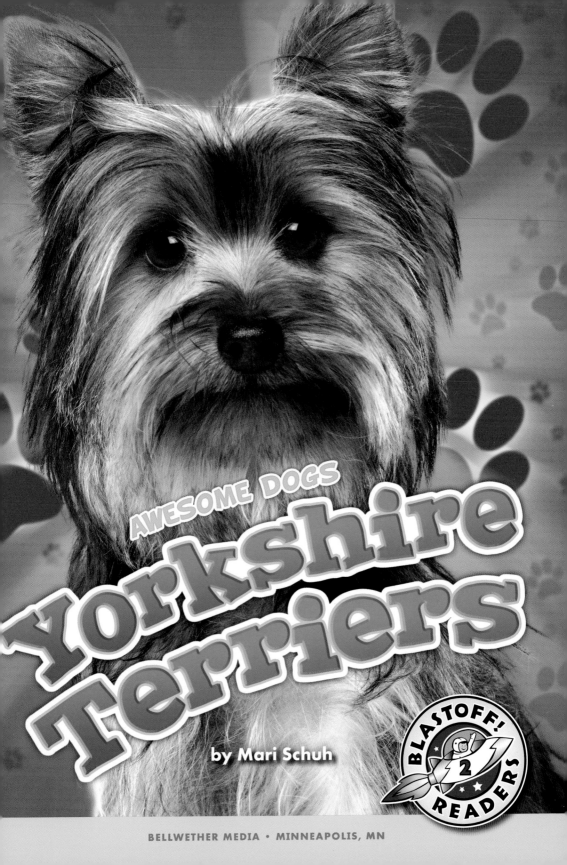

AWESOME DOGS

Yorkshire Terriers

by Mari Schuh

BELLWETHER MEDIA • MINNEAPOLIS, MN

BLASTOFF!
2
READERS

Note to Librarians, Teachers, and Parents:

Blastoff! Readers are carefully developed by literacy experts and combine standards-based content with developmentally appropriate text.

Level 1 provides the most support through repetition of high-frequency words, light text, predictable sentence patterns, and strong visual support.

Level 2 offers early readers a bit more challenge through varied simple sentences, increased text load, and less repetition of high-frequency words.

Level 3 advances early-fluent readers toward fluency through increased text and concept load, less reliance on visuals, longer sentences, and more literary language.

Level 4 builds reading stamina by providing more text per page, increased use of punctuation, greater variation in sentence patterns, and increasingly challenging vocabulary.

Level 5 encourages children to move from "learning to read" to "reading to learn" by providing even more text, varied writing styles, and less familiar topics.

Whichever book is right for your reader, Blastoff! Readers are the perfect books to build confidence and encourage a love of reading that will last a lifetime!

This edition first published in 2016 by Bellwether Media, Inc.

No part of this publication may be reproduced in whole or in part without written permission of the publisher. For information regarding permission, write to Bellwether Media, Inc., Attention: Permissions Department, 5357 Penn Avenue South, Minneapolis, MN 55419.

Library of Congress Cataloging-in-Publication Data

Schuh, Mari C., 1975- author.
  Yorkshire Terriers / by Mari Schuh.
    pages cm. – (Blastoff! Readers. Awesome Dogs)
  Summary: "Relevant images match informative text in this introduction to Yorkshire terriers. Intended for students in kindergarten through third grade"– Provided by publisher.
  Audience: Ages 5-8
  Audience: K to grade 3
  Includes bibliographical references and index.
  ISBN 978-1-62617-244-9 (hardcover : alk. paper)
  1. Yorkshire terrier–Juvenile literature. 2. Dogs–Juvenile literature. I. Title.
  SF429.Y6S38 2016
  636.76–dc23
                              2015011008

Printed in the United States of America, North Mankato, MN.

Table of Contents

What Are Yorkshire Terriers?

Yorkshire terriers are one of the smallest dog **breeds**. They are also called Yorkies.

These tiny dogs are busy and bold.

Yorkies weigh 7 pounds
(3 kilograms) or less.

Yorkshire Terrier Profile

V-shaped ears

small body

long, silky hair

Life Span: 12 to 15 years

Trainability:

| 1 | 2 | 3 | 4 | 5 | 6 |

Hardest to train   Easiest to train

Their small size puts them in the **Toy Group** of the **American Kennel Club**.

Silky Coats

Yorkies have fine, **silky** hair.
Their **coats** feel like human hair.

and black hair. The black turns
gray as the puppies grow.

topknot
↓

Some Yorkies have short haircuts.
Others have long, straight hair.
Their legs and feet are hidden.

Yorkshire Terrier Hairstyles

short hair

long hair

Many Yorkies wear a **topknot**. It keeps hair out of their eyes.

History of Yorkshire Terriers

Yorkies came from other terrier breeds.

Scotland

Yorkshire, England

In the mid-1800s, some workers in Scotland moved to Yorkshire, England. They brought small terriers with them.

The workers' terriers had puppies with local terriers. These new Yorkshire terriers hunted rats in clothing mills.

Some Yorkies take part in **agility** events. They run through tunnels. They also jump and climb.

Yorkies enjoy being around people. They like to cuddle.

They are always ready for fun. Many Yorkies travel with their owners.

These brave little dogs are tough and **rugged**.

Yorkies are not afraid to stand up to bigger dogs. This can get them into trouble!

Glossary

agility—a dog sport where dogs run through a series of obstacles

American Kennel Club—an organization that keeps track of dog breeds in the United States

breeds—types of dogs

coats—the hair or fur covering some animals

rugged—strong and rough

silky—soft, smooth, and shiny

spunky—full of spirit and courage

topknot—a knot of hair at the top of the head tied with a bow or ribbon

Toy Group—a group of the smallest dog breeds; most dogs in the Toy Group were bred to be companions.

To Learn More

AT THE LIBRARY
Beal, Abigail. *I Love My Yorkshire Terrier*. New York, N.Y.: PowerKids Press, 2011.

George, Charles and Linda. *Yorkshire Terrier*. New York, N.Y.: Children's Press, 2010.

Shores, Erika L. *All About Yorkshire Terriers*. North Mankato, Minn.: Capstone Press, 2013.

ON THE WEB
Learning more about Yorkshire terriers is as easy as 1, 2, 3.

1. Go to www.factsurfer.com.

2. Enter "Yorkshire terriers" into the search box.

3. Click the "Surf" button and you will see a list of related web sites.

With factsurfer.com, finding more information is just a click away.

Index

The images in this book are reproduced through the courtesy of: Eric Isselee, front cover, p. 11 (left); Sergey Lavrentev, p. 4; Imageman, p. 5; Nneirda, p. 6; Ermolaev Alexander, p. 7; scorpp, p. 8; Hal P, p. 9; Klein-Hubert/ Kimball Stock, p. 10; dien, p. 11 (right); Angela Hampton Picture Library/ Alamy, p. 12; Silke Klewitz-Seeman/ Corbis, p. 14; Hill Street Studios/ Glow Images, p. 15; tsik, p. 16; Mark Herreid, p. 17; Felix Mizioznikov, p. 18; alexkatkov, p. 19; Tierfotoagentur/ S. Schwerdtfeger/ Age Fotostock, p. 20; Alexandra Pfau/ Glow Images, p. 21.